NUMBER 461

THE ENGLISH
EXPERIENCE

ITS RECORD IN EARLY PRINTED BOOKS
PUBLISHED IN FACSIMILE

The publishers acknowledge their gratitude to
the Curators of the Bodleian Library, Oxford
for their permission to reproduce the
Library's copy, Shelfmark: Wood 594 (2)

Library of Congress Catalog Card Number:
75-38190

S.T.C.No. 12058

Collation: [ ]^1, B-G^4

Published in 1972 by

Theatrvm Orbis Terrarvm Ltd.,
O.Z.Voorburgwal 85, Amsterdam

&

Da Capo Press Inc.
-a subsidiary of Plenum Publishing Corporation-
277 West 17th Street, New York N.Y. 10011

Printed in the Netherlands
ISBN 90 221 0461 3

England and Scotlands Happineſſe.

In being reduced to vnitie of Religion, vnder our invincible Monarke King Iames.

Written by J: Gordon.

Printed at London by V.S. for William Aſpley, and are by him to be ſold at his ſhop in Paules Church-yard,
1 6 0 4.

A Panegyrique of Congratula-
tion for the concord of the realmes
of great Brittaine, in vnitie of religion
vnder one King.

 N auncient writer faith,
that the ground and main-
tenance of all Monar-
chies and Empires is con-
cord, their ruine and fub-
uerfion is difcorde . The
Hiftories of things paft for
fixteene hundred yeeres,
fince the eternall Sonne of God and Monarke of
all Monarkes, became man to redeeme fuch as
fhould beleeue in him, fhew vs many fayre and
admirable bleffings which God hath powred vppon the Ilands of great Brittaine, and the planting of Chriftian truth in them, the which I will
reprefent vnto your Maieftie, to fhew plainly that
the cócord & vnionof the people, & nations ouer
             B   whom

whom God hath made you King, is the accomplifhment and perfection of all the precedent benefites which his diuine bountie hath beftowed vppon the people vnder your moft happie gouernment.

The Apoftle Saint *Peter* in his firft Catholike Epiftle the fecond Chapter, fayeth that Chriftians are; *a chofen race, a royall Priefthoode, a holy nation, a people purchafed to God as his owne*. The which is very fitly applied to the people vnder your commaunde, feeing that God hath firft vnited them vnder this royaltie and Priefthoode of Chriftian veritie, and afterwardes hath vfed this vnion of their foules, as a Mother to bring foorth the vnion of three Realmes vnder your Maieftie in one royaltie. The fayde Apoftle in the fame place doth teach vs to what ende God hath placed vs in this happie concorde, That is: *To the ende (fayeth he) that you fhoulde declare his vertues, who hath called you out of darkeneffe to his admirable light*. The which fhould mooue vs to preferre the wonderfull workes of God, before all worldly things, who hauing freede and redeemed vs from darkeneffe, from inuocation and adoration of deade men, and from Pagan Idolatrie, wherein our predeceffours haue beene fo long abufed (worfhipping Images, and the vifible formes of Creatures, as the Creator himfelfe and the crea-

creature infteade of the Creator) hath fince
and in this latter age , called and infpired vs
to woifhippe him the onely Creator of all
things.

Moreouer the Apoftle in the fame place doeth
fhewe vs what man was before, that is, *Before
you were no people , and now you are the people of
God : you had not obtayned mercie, but now you
haue obteyned mercie*. The people (S I R E)of the
Ilands of great Brittaine , were not vnited in religion, in peace, in concorde , in like affections
and will vnder one King, but they haue beene
long banded one agaynft an other , in a Sea
of difcordes, difcentions, and cruell warres,
againft the decree and lawe of God , for that
they were out of Chriftian charitie , hauing
no other obiect in their foules but hatred
and malice , with a defire of reuenge , and fo
by confequence they were not Gods people, but
caft-awayes , by reafon of their Idolatrie and
fpirituall fornication wherewith they were po-
luted, and fo vnworthy to obtayne mercie.
But now that the light of the Gofpell , the true
worfhippe of one God hath taken liuely and
fure roote in their hartes vnder the fortunate
raygne of the deceafed Queene , and vnder your
happy and lawefull fucceffion in thefe Realmes,
they are become of one heart, of one affection , and finally beeing made the true people

of God, they haue obtained blessing, grace and mercie.

The comicall Poet sayth. *A King is the image of the liuing God.* Christian diuinity teacheth vs that in God, there be three persõs vnited in one deytie essence and power. *Saint Augustine* compares the Trinity to the three partes of a mans soule, which are distinguished in opperations and functions vnited in one and the same essence. I beseech God (S I R E) so to worke in the hartes of your subiects, and in the three realmes vnited vnder the power, and commaund of your royall Maiesty, that beeing bound togeather, they may represent the three persons of the Triniyte in one deity, and that agreeing in one will vnder your Monarchy, they may be made the true image of the heauenly, that all may bee one in Christ as Christ is one with his father.

It was neuer seene in any age, that the nations of the Ilands of *Brittanie,* were vnited in hart and affection vnder one King , as the admirable power of God hath lately brought them vnder your maiesty: whereof the true and onely cause is the purity and truth of Christian religion : the which God of his especial grace hath miraculously planted in your realmes, and sence continued in you, causing you to be borne the lawfull and vndoubted heire of these three auncient Imperiall Crowns of the west, to raigne Christianly, peace-
ably

ably and happily as vndoubtedly you shall, seeing that God hath indued and beautified you with learning in aboundance, and so great wisdome, as I may iustly say these vertues surpasse the greatnes of your royall maiesty.

If we examine the order of Histories, we shall obserue, that this most happy vnion of English and Scottish vnder one King, hath beene long before foreseene by the diuine prouidence, to be finally effected in our age by the establishment of the ancient Christian religion in your Ilands, and the abolishion of the new religion of *Arrius*, *Nestorius*, and *Eutichius* brought in by the Stratagems of the olde serpent, the spirite of errour and darkenesse through the ministry of Popes, who since sixe hundred yeeres, vnder the name of Christianity, haue built vp againe this pagan idolatry, hauing changed the Bishops and pastors of the Church into worldly power, vsurping vpon the Kings of the Westerne Empire, in whose soules (through superstition and ignorance of the Christian truth) they haue planted a more insupportable tyrannye, then that which auncient Rome had conquered by force of armes.

The great God of armies hath (in your Maiesties person) begun this happy vnion and concord betwixt two nations, which had for so many ages beene in cruell and bloudy warres, that

you might imploye the valour of their armes
for the deliuery of his church, from the bar-
barous tyranny wherewith fhee hath beene long
oppreffed by Popes . And as *Conftantine* the
great, the protector and reftorer of the auncient
Chriftian Church, was borne in great *Brittaine,*
and there beganne his Empire, obtayning afterwardes admirable victories againft fowre Romaine Tyrantes perfecutors of the Church of
God, by meanes whereof he did abolifh Gen-
tilifme, and planted Chriftian Religion at Rome
and throughout the Empire . In like forte the
fame God hath raifed your Maieftie to the height
of greatneffe, to be fucceffor vnto *ConStantine* in
the faide Realmes, and to chafe out of the fame
Rome the idolatry and abhomination of the
Gentiles, the which Sathan hath fence brought
in vnder the name of Chrift, which is the true
meanes to purchafe you the iuft title of protector and defender of the faith and reftorer of
Chriftianitie . And as God by that marriage
of *Henrie* the feauenth with *Elizabeth* his wife
made the Vnion of the houfes of *Lancafter* and
Yorke, who had a long time beene in bloudye
warres, and by the marriage of *Iames* the fourth
King of *Scotland* with *Marguerite* the eldeft
daughter of the fayde *Henrie* the feauenth your
great graundfather, the coniunction of the
crownes of *England* and *Scotland* within thefe
hun-

hundred yeares : So wee hope that the fame God will imploye this admirable Vnion vnder your commaunde to vnite the Chriftian and v-niuerfall Church vnder one fpirituall royalty, which is the worfhip of one God, and to abolifh idolatry, which hath in a maner fwallowed vp and deuoured the true Church.

My intention is to reprefent in briefe vnto your Maiefty and to all Chriftians defirous of eternall health, the infinite graces & benifits which God hath powred vpon your Ilands, in the planting & maintaining the preaching of his Gofpell, that it may plainely appeare, that neither the deceafed Queene *Elizabeth* of happy memory, nor your Maiefty haue eftablifhed any new religion in your Ilands, but banifhed the new, being polluted and defiled with errours and falfe worfhippes of the *Gentiles, Arians, Neftorians,* and *Eutichians,* & that the Religion which dooth now flourifh in your Realmes, is the fame which foone after the death of our Sauiour was preached and receaued by the Kings your predeceflours, and by the people of your Realmes.

Theodoret a Greeke bifhop and one of the moft ancient of the Church in his bookes *de curatione Grecarum affectionum, fermon 9. de legibus,* makes a goodly comparifon betwixt the power of the Romaine Empire, and their Lawes, & the Empire of Iefus Chrift, and of his Lawe receiued

through-

8

throughout the worlde. He faieth, the *Romaines* could neuer make the *Perfians* and *Parthians* of the Eaſt ſubieƈt to their lawes, nor towardes the North, the *Cimbrians, Danes*, nor the people of *Brittaine*. But the power of Ieſus Chriſt hath beene greater, for (faieth he) our fiſherman that is Saint *Peter*, and our maker of tents, which is Saint *Paul*, haue made the Brittiſh people ſubieƈt to the lawes of Chriſt, the which would not o-bey the Romaine lawes, ſo as antiquitie doth te-ſtifie that the Apoſtles haue preached in our I-lands. *Metaphraſtes* (cited by the Cardinall *Baro-nius*) ſayeth that Saint *Peter* came thether. *Ioſeph* of *Arimathie*, and *Simon Zelotes* came likewiſe, as Hiſtories do teach vs. This ſeede of the Goſpell in your Ilands tooke ſuch increaſe, as King *Lucius* and all his ſubieƈts, about the yeere 180. did pub-likely receiue the Chriſtian religion.

Baleus ex Gilda et a-lys ſcript. Anglis.Ni-ceph.l.2.c 4

And indeede the *Chronographers* haue noted that about the yeare of our Lord 180.*Brittaine* was the firſt part of the world which did publiquely receiue the fayth of Chriſt, for *Lucius* King of *Brittaine* did in thoſe dayes depoſe the Prieſts of the Gentiles, and did ſubſtitute in their places Biſhoppes and Chriſtian paſtors; hee baniſhed Gentiliſme out of his countrie, which hapned not in any part of the worlde, vntill the time of *Conſtantine* the great.*Tertulian,* and *Origen* who liued about the ſame time teſtifie, that the coun-tries

Plat. in vit.The: leſph.

tries of *Brittaine* beeing inacceſſible for the *Ro-mains* were ſubieƈt vnto Chriſt. The Biſhops of this Iland were at the councell of *Nice*, held vnder *Conſtantine* the great, three hundred yeares after Chriſt, which is the firſt period of Chriſtianiſme, during the which the Chriſtians did ſuffer twelue moſt cruell perſecutions vnder the tyrannie of Paganiſme and the Idolatrie of olde *Rome*.

We well wot that during the three firſt Periods of Chriſtianitie, whereof eyther conteynes three hundred yeares, the true and onely worſhippe of one God, which hath beene planted ſince the Apoſtles time in your Ilands, hath beene continued there during the ſaid time, and yet the Chriſtians, which liued in thoſe ages (no not the *Romaines*) did euer allowe (in the publique vſe of the ſeruice of the Church,) of the worſhip of the hoſt in the Romiſh maſſe, nor of the pretended woode of the very croſſe, nor of the Images of Ieſus Chriſt, or his ſepulcher ſeated neare to Mount *Caluarie*, all which are worſhiped in the new Romiſh Church as God himſelfe, which worſhips are abhominations of the *Gentils*, *Arriens* & *Neſtoriens*, which bring with it the ſhipwracke of eternall health.

The Chriſtians vvhich liued during the firſt Period of the three hundred yeares of Chriſtianitie, did inuiolably keepe the firſt commaunde-

C   ment

ment . *Thou shalt haue no other Gods against my face, or before mee*, which the *Thargum* of the *Caldeans* hath interpreted, *besides mee, or any other then mee.* The *Greeke* tranflation faith, *other Gods besides me. Athanasius* interpreting this commaundement fayth, *Hee hath not forbidden them to haue other Gods, for that there were other Gods, but leaft any one falling from the true God, should make him a God of that which is not, like to thofe Gods which the Poets and writers make mention of, which haue but the name of God and not the effect.* And the fame Authour fayeth, *If reafon and the efteeme we houlde of God doth make vs beleeue that hee may bee in all places, and that nothing of all that which God hath vnder him is God, and that all things are vnder his power, why doe not they which make a creature God, fee, that it is out of the definition attributed vnto God.*

Athanaf.
Orat. cont.
gentes.tom.
1. pag. 34.

Theodoret vppon the fame commaundement faith, that the *Arrians* offend againft it, and the true Chriftians obferue it . They doe not allowe any thing to be held or worfhiped for God, but the deuine nature : but thofe which follow the error of *Arrius* and *Eunomius*, finne directly againft the deuine law, for they confeffe the onely Sonne of God, but they maintaine that he was created and is deuided from the deuine fubftance . God hauing fayde , *Thou shalt haue no other Gods but me*, doubtleffe thefe men bring in another God.

By

By thefe authorities we do inferre,that the Romains which worfhip the hoft in the Maffe,breake this commaundement,for they agree,that it is no part of the deuine nature,but of the fubftance and nature of Iefus Chrifts humanitie, who is worfhiped according to his diuinitie,and not after his humanitie, according to the auncient fimboles of the Church. The Chriftian faith then hath for a firme and onely foundation the worfhip of one God,according to this firft commaundement,and the worfhip of any thing created by God, which is vnder him,ought not to be receiued in the Chriftian religion, but the onely deuine nature of the Father,Sonne,and holy Ghoft, ought to be worfhiped and called on in Triple vnitie, without the which nothing ought to be worfhiped, without manifeft impietie and idolatrie.

The fame *Theodoret* interpreting this commandement, faieth, *Serm. 2.* God the maker of all things in the beginning of the law which he gaue vnto *Mofes* cōmaunded him to worfhip one God. *I am*(faith he) *the Lord thy God, which brought thee out of the land of Egypt,* & whē he hath put *Mofes* in mind of his late benefits, he exhorts him to perfift in the feruice of god,not to deuide his worfhip but to cleaue onely vnto God, *Thou fhalt not* (faith he) *haue any other Gods but me.*The which doth teach vs that thofe of the Komifh corruptiō haue brought in ftrange Gods, for that they haue deuided the

adorati-

adoration and veneration betwixt God and his creatures, making three degrees. The firſt they call *Latria*, which they attribute to God and to the *Hoſt* in the Maſſe equally. The ſecond *Hyperdeulia*, which they yeelde to the bleſſed virgin. And the third *Dulia*, attributed to their other *Saints* and to their images and reliques, abuſing with too groſſe an ignorance the ſignification of theſe *Greeke* wordes, for *Deulia* ſignifies a greater ſeruice then *Latria*. And we learne that in this place *Theodoret* calles the ſeruice and adoration of God, by the name of *Deulia*, and ſo doe *Athanaſius* and *Chriſoſtome*. And Saint *Auguſtine* who hath brought in this diſtinction, attributes both vnto God onely. *In his 84. Queſtion vpon Exod.*

Iuſtin Martir who liued vnder *Antonius Pius* in the ſecond age of this period of Chriſtianity, ſhewes plainely that the Chriſtians did not alow of the worſhip of any thing inferiour to the *Deity*, and ſaieth that Ieſus Chriſt had ſo taught them : for ſpeaking to the Emperour in his Apologie for the Chriſtians of his time, hee writes thus. That God onely is to be worſhipped, for ſo Chriſt doth teach the greateſt commandement is, *thou ſhalt worſhippe the Lorde thy God, and him onely ſhalt thou honour with all thy heart and all thy ſtrength, the Lorde God which hath created thee.* And a little after he ſaith, we worſhip
God

God onely , in other things we willingly ſerue
you, for that we do acknowledge you for Kings
and Princes of men, and we pray vnto God that
he will giue you wiſedome equall to your royall
power. So as the Chriſtians in matters of religion
did not yeeld any worſhip to things created, neither did they deuide the worſhip betwixt God &
his creatures, as the Romiſh Church doth.

Many Chriſtians of the ſame time, were ſo ex-
act obſeruers of the onely worſhippe of God , as
they would not reuerence the Roman Emperors,
as the ſouldiers did in ciuil cauſes, for *Theophilus*
to *Apoſtolicus* the ſixt Biſhop of *Antioche* , who
liued in the yeare of our Lord 173. when as *Luci-*
us was King of great *Brittaine*; ſaith I ſhall honor
the Emperour more in praying for him , then in
worſhipping him, for it is not lawfull to worſhip
any but God onely.

The Chriſtians of theſe three firſt ages , had
no Alters, no Images, nor any materiall croſſes of
golde, ſiluer, wood, or ſtone , for *Clemens Alexan-*
drinus who was neere the Apoſtles time ſaith.
Wee Chriſtians are expreſlye forbidden to vſe *In Parene-*
any arte of deceite (for ſo hee calleth painting *tico.*
and making of Images) Thou ſhalt not (ſaith the
Prophet *Moſes*) make the likeneſſe of any thing
that is in heauen aboue, or on the earth beneath.
And the ſame author *Strom. Lib. 5. Pythagoras* (ſaith
he) forbids the wearing of rings , nor to ingraue

in

in them the images and figures of Gods, as *Mo-fes* had long before forbidden, and that we muft not make any Image, be it grauen, molten, counterfeite or painted, that wee fhould not bee carryed away with fenfible things, but fhould paffe vnto thofe thinges which are comprehended by vnderftanding, And foone after he faith; To honour the effence by the knowledge of a materiall thing, is to contemne it.

The Doctrine of the Romifh Church dooth heerein directly oppugne the Doctrine of Chriftian antiquitye, making a new God of the hoft of the new Maffe, giuing it the name of God, worfhipping it as God, and yet their doctors confeffe that it is made and created by the wordes of confecration.

It is therefore euident that they haue brought into the Church a God created, which is not contayned in the definition of God, before mentioned by Saint *Athanafius*, for the hoaft of the Maffe is not euerye where, which is the property of God onelye, neither dooth it containe all things vnder his power : but contrarywife the Counfell of *Trent* faith in expreffe wordes, that Iefus Chrift God and man is contained vnder the vifibie fignes of Breade, of Wine, which is quite contrarye to the diuine nature, which contaynes all things in it,

and

and is not contained in anye thing . The God therefore of the Romish Maſſe, is a God created which hath a beginning and ending, and is contained in the viſible forme of Breade and Wine, and containes not in it all things crea-ted ; ſo as the worſhippers of this God of the Maſſe, doe worſhippe a newe and ſtrange God , contrarye to the firſt commaunde-ment.

If the *Arrians* (as *Theodoret* ſaith) haue bro-ken this firſt commaundement , for that they taught that Ieſus Chriſt according to his deity was a creature, and yet he was God, with grea-ter reaſon the Romaines tranſgreſſe the ſame commaundement, confeſſing that the preten-ded deitie of the hoaſt of the Maſſe, is a deitie purchaſed by the conſecration, and not by the eternall deity, without beginning and without ending . And the ſame *Theodoret* writing againſt the Greekes in the foreſaide paſſage, teacheth vs, that by the commaundement which ſaith . *Thou ſhalt haue no other Gods but mee* , that *Moſes* forbiddes to make anye deuiſion of the de-uine worſhippe, but to giue all to God one-lye. The Romaines who haue made three de-grees of worſhipping , cannot denie but they haue broken this firſt commaundement , and brought in a multitude of Gods , making as manye Gods as they ſaye Maſſes : So as

C 4   their

their pluralitie of Gods becomes infinite, and
furpaffeth the multitude of the *Paynims* Gods.
Minutius Fœlix,Tertulian,Origen,and *Arnobius,*
who liued in the third age of this firlt Periode of
Chriftianifme, teftifie that the *Gentiles* accufed
the Chriftians,for that they had neither Temples,
Altars,Images, nor vifible or Materiall Sacrifices,
and that they did hide from fight,that which they
did worfhippe. *Cecilius* a Pagan Oratour, difpu-
ting againft *Octauius* a Chriftian, as *Minutius*
doth reporte, obieded to the Chriftians. *Why
haue they no Alters, no Temples, no knowne Images.* They did blazon our Chriftians in the wor-
fhiping of the Croffe,which they fayd they de-
ferued, taking the Croffe for a punifhment. To
whom *Octauius* aunfweres for the Chriftians. *We
neither worfhippe nor defire Croffes, but you who haue
confecrated Gods of Wood,worfhiping Croffes of Wood,
as peeces of your Gods.*Whereby it appeares that the
auncient Chriftians in the pureneffe of Chriftian
religion did neither worfhip croffes of Gold, Siluer, Stone orWood, as thefe doe of the Romifh
religion. How fhould they I pray you worfhippe
them, feing they had them not?& which is more,
would not haue them ? But the Church of *Rome*
doth quite contrarie,running after Gods of Gold
and Siluer, made (as the *Pfalmet* faieth) by mans
hand.

In regarde of that which the *Gentiles* did obiect
vnto

vnto the Chriſtians, that they did hide, and not
ſhew forth what they did worſhip. *Octauius* aun-
ſweres for the Chriſtians. *Doe you thinke that we
doe hide what we do worſhip, although we haue neither
Temples, nor Aulters? for what Image ſhall I make of
God? If thou haſt thy right ſences, thou ſhalt finde
that man is the true Image of God.* And a little after
he ſaith : *But the God whom we worſhip, we neither
ſhewe nor ſee.* If the auncient Chriſtians had beene
like vnto the Romiſh Chriſtians of this age, the
Gentiles could not haue obiected, that they had
neither Aultars nor Images : for in truth they
haue more Aulters and Images then the Gentiles
had. Neither ſhould they haue obiected vnto the
Chriſtiãs, that they concealed what they worſhipped, for the Romains ſhew in the eleuation of the
Hoſt, the God which they worſhip, & cauſe the
people to worſhip it, the which they not onely
ſhewe in Temples, but alſo in the ſtreetes, and
in generall proceſſions, and other ſolemnities, they
ſhew forth what they worſhip, againſt the vſe of
the firſt Chriſtians.

Tertulian in his booke of Idolatrie, confutes
with many reaſons, the making of all ſortes of
Images, to roote out all matter of Idolatrie; and
after he had cited the ſecond commaundement,
whereby it is defended to make the likeneſſe of
anie thing that is in heauen or earth, hee ſaith, *It
is forbidden throughout all the worlde, for the ſeruants*

D   *of*

of God to vse such making of Images, seeing that
Enoch *had foretoulde that the Diuell or the Angels*
of darkeneſſe ſhould turne all the Elements into Iaola-
trie, and all that is conteyned in Heauen and Earth,
that all theſe things might bee conſecrated for God
againſt God himſelfe. And ſo mans errour doth
worſhippe all things except the Creator of all things.
Their Images were Idols, and the conſecration of I-
mages is Idolatrie. And whatſoeuer Idolatrie com-
mits, muſt neceſſarily be attributed to the maker of the
Idol.

That which *Origen* ſpeaketh vpon the Epiſtle
to the *Romaines,*is to be conſidered,to make Chriſtians wholy to reiect Idolatrie: For after that he
hath refuted the Errours of the *Gentiles,* in that
they might know God by the viſible Ellementes,
yet they had fallen to the worſhippe of the
viſible Images of Creatures, concluding thus.
To the ende that in fewe wordes wee may ſpeake the
truth, wee houlde it an abhominable impietie to
worſhippe any thing, except the Father, Sonne, and
holy Ghoſt.

And a little after hee ſaith, *They wrong them-*
ſelues that ſerue Images, and worſhippe the Creature
leauing the Creator : But we Chriſtians which wor-
ſhip and adore the Father,Sonne,and holy Ghoſt onely,
and no other Creature, as we doe not erre in the di-
uine worſhippe,ſo doe wee not offend in our actions and
conuerſation. It is moſt certaine that the Hoſt offred

vp

vp in the *Romaine Lyturgie*, is not confubftantiall
with theFather,Son,& holy Ghoft, & much leffe
vnited in confubftantialitie with the Trinitie,as it
is well noted in the fermon *de Cæna Domini*, infer-
ted among the workes of *Cyprian* who liued in
the third age, where it is faide. *That the diuine ef-*
fence is infufed in the vifible Sacrament after an vn-
fpeakable manner, that there might bee more deuoti-
on and reuerence giuen to the Sacraments, and a more
holy acceffe to the truth of him, of whofe bodie they
bee Sacraments, and to the participating of the fpi-
rite, not to the confubftantialitie of Chrift, but to
this brotherly and indiuifible vnitie : for the Sonne
onely is confubftantiall with the Father, the fub-
ftance of the Trinitie may not bee deuided, our
coniunction, and that of Chrift doth not confounde
the perfons, nor vnite the fubftances, but doth onely
confociate the affections, and binde the willes. If in
the perfon of Iefus Chrift, confifting of three
natures in one perfon, worfhiped with one onely worfhippe : the deuine nature had beene onely infufed in the humanitie of Iefus Chrift after his birth, as *Neftorius* did teach, and not
vnited perfonally in the virgins wombe.

Cyrillus and the other *Orthodoxes* did right-
ly mainetaine agaynft him, that to worfhippe
one Chrift carrying God in him, had beene an
Antropolatrie or Pagan Idolatrie . With greater
reafon the infufion of the Diuinitie in the

Sacrament

Sacrament and in the elements of Breade and Wine,cannot attribute vnto it the dignity to bee worshipped as God himselfe,for (as that text doth teach vs) this infusion which is made in the sacrament is not consubstantiall with the deity of the Sonne of God,the which is onely consubstantiall with the father and the holy spirite, for that it dooth affect a most straight and mutuall coniunction betwixt God and vs. Saint *Iohn* in his seuenteenth Chapter speaketh of this coniunction and vnion, where our Sauiour prayes to his father for all those that shall beleeue in him . *That all may be one,as thou O father art in me, and I in thee, that they may be one in vs.*If this vnion should make that sacrament of the Lords supper to be worshipped, then those which are vnited in Christ,and by him in God the father, should worship one another, for our Sauiour saith in the sixt of Saint *Iohn. Hee that eates my flesh and drinks my bloud,remaines in me & I in him.*That we might know (saith *Cypriā*)*that our abiding in him is a true eating, and the drinking an incorporation, with a duty of obedience, ioyning of willes and vnitie of affections.* The eating therefore is a certaine greedinesse in vs, and a desire to remaine for euer in Christ.

We learne by these authorities, that euen as Chrifts abyding in vs by our eating of the sacrament,makes vs not capable of worship,for that by this coniunction wee are not perfonally vnited
with

with the deity of Iesus Chrift, In like fort the infufion of the deuine effence in the facramentes,
whereof Saint *Cyprian* fpeakes, makes not the fa-
crament to be worfhipped, if it were fo, the faid a-
doration were in idolatrye like that of *Neftorius*,
who worfhipped man carrying God in him, as is
faid before.

We may therfore fay with good reafon againft
thofe that worfhip the creatures, and the images
of Iefus Chrift, his fepulcher, and the wood of
the croffe, that which *Origen* fpeaketh againft the
Gentiles of his time. *God is the vertue which go-*
uernes all things, and the diuinitye which filleth all
things, making themfelues thereby inexcufable, that
whereas God hath giuen them the grace to know him
yet haue they not honoured him as they ought, neither
haue they giuen him due thankes, but haue fought in
the vanity of their owne imaginations the images of
God. As thofe of the Romifh Church doe in the
Maffe, for in their hoaft they make figures and
images. They haue loft in themfelues the I-
mage of God : they which vanted to haue
the fpirite of wifedome, are fallen into the ob-
fcure darkeneffe of ignorance. For what is there
more abhominable thé to turne the glory of God
to the corporall and corruptible image of mans
nature? the which is done at this prefent throughout all the Romifh Church as it is faide. So as
they haue conuerted God the Creatour of all

things

things, into a corporall and corruptible forme,
whome they thought to worſhip vnder thoſe viſible formes, wee wִll thereſore conclude our
diſcourſe of the proofe of the true and onely a-
doration of God, obſerued throughout all the
habitable world, during the firſt periode of three
hundred yeares, with the teſtimonye of *Arno-*
bius, writing againſt the Gentiles obiecting to
the Chriſtians, that they would not worſhippe
any but the firſt, and the greateſt of all the Gods,
and not the interiour Gods , according to the
manner in thoſe dayes, to whome hee aunſwe-
reth ſaying. *And wee may ſay in that which concernes*
the worſhippe and honour of the diuinity, that it ſuffi-
ceth vs to haue one onelye God , God I ſaye the father
of all things, who hath created and gouerneth all things.
In worſhipping of him wee worſhippe all that we ought
to worſhippe, when wee honour him, wee honour in
him that which hee requires at our handes , what
the duety of worſhippe dooth exaƈt, that we performe
by our worſhippe . For ſeeing wee holde the chieſe
of all diuinitye, of whome all diuine thinges depend,
wee thinke it ſuperfluous to ſeeke to priuate perſons.
And a little after hee ſaithe : *As in earthlye king-*
domes wee are not conſtrained to worſhippe and ho-
nour euerye priuate man of the Kings houſe, but in
the honour wee doe vnto Kings , thoſe which be-
*long vnto them are ſeeretly honored with them.*So the
Chri-

Chriſtians of that perfect age, did not worſhippe nor call vpon any thing vnder God, as
the Romaniſtes of our age doe, which worſhip
the bleſſed virgin , the Angelles *Michael* and
Gabriel , Saint *Iohn Baptiſt*, the Apoſtles and
Martyrs , their reliques , Sepulchers and Images . So as it is moſt apparent that the Religion
planted at this preſent in the Ilandes of great
Brittaine is the true auncient Religion , and the
only worſhip of one God, incômunicable to the
Creatures, the which hath continued during the
firſt periode of the three hundred yeares of Chriſtianity . So as it is a meere ſlander what the aduerſaries of the trueth ſaye , that your Maieſtye
hath baniſhed the true auncient Chriſtian Religion out of your Realmes, to plant a newe Religion , pretended to bee begunne by *Martin
Luther*, *Iohn Caluin*, and other great Perſona-
ges in the puritye of the true Chriſtian Doctrine.

But contrarywiſe it is an immortall glorye
which ſhall increaſe in your raigne , and continue to poſterity, ſeeing that your Maieſty is the
author of the reſtoring of the true Chriſtian religion in your realmes, hauing reſtored it I ſaye to
that beauty and ſincerity, as it was in oulde time
planted by *Lucius* your fore-runner , the firſt
Chriſtian King of great *Brittayne* , who

be-

became so affectionate and zealous of the advancement and propagation of the trueth, and so great an enemie to Idolatrie and the worship of Creatures and visible formes, that of a King he became a Preacher (as some Histories say) And as during the persecutiō of the Christians vnder *Dioclesian* and *Maxentius* which were the most bloudie of all, God vsed your Ilands and kingdomes as a refuge for the true Christians which fled from the saide persecutions; Euen so the same God hath made your most happie raigne to be a safe harbour for the Christians of our age, who haue been forced to abandon houses, goods, and inheritances, rather then to bow to the Romish worship.

God the protector of his true Church hath continued his admirable graces ouer your Ilands in the second Period of Christianisme, the which begun with the most happie Empire of *Constantius Chlorus*: for during the last persecution, God rayſed vp this wise and warlike Emperour in the westerne parts of Europe, in the which *England*, *Scotland*, and *Ireland*, are conteyned, where the saide Emperor tooke to wife *Hellen*, borne in your said realmes, who receiued into his protection all the Christians which fled from other prouinces to auoyde the cruell persecution which was made againſt them by his other associates in the Empire. S I R E, we must here obserue a notable pollicie of this wise Emperour, to trie the fidelitie of his

Euseb.in vita Constan.

ser-

feruants and minifters in the gouernment of his
Empire,which will much auaile for the preferua-
tion of your royall eftate. He did publifh a fayned
edict, commaunding all the fubiects of his Empire to facrifice to the falfe Gods, and whofoeuer
fhould refufe fo to doe, to departe out of his armies and Empire. This proclamation beeing
made a great number of Chriftians, did facrifice
vnto the falfe Gods,to preferue their eftates, dig-
nities, and goods : but the true Chriftians defired
rather to leaue all, then to ferue them, where-
vpon the Emperour difcouered himfelfe prefent-
ly,and difcharged all fuch as had worfhiped thefe
falfe Gods: faying,*How can they be faithful vnto the* *Idem in*
Emperour, that are faithleffe vnto God? And as for *Conftant.*
the true Chriftians which had left all, hee called
them home and made them guardiens both of his
perfon and eftate, as *Eufebius* faith. I defire not
your Maieftie fhould make fuch counterfeite pro-
clamations, but that the fame God which hath
made you fucceffor to *Conftantius Chlorus*, will
giue you the grace to make fuch an election of
your fubiects, as in your moft important affaires
you admit not any but fuch as are knowne to be
well grounded in the true Chriftian religion. For
euen as a modeft woman ought not onely to
be chaft, but free from all fufpition, euen fo
thofe which are imployed in the affaires of true
Chriftian Princes,(as your Maieftie is) fhould be
E free

free from all fuſpition of falſe religion. The ſaid *Conſtantius* died at Yorke in England, after that hee had inſtituted *Conſtantine* the great his ſonne, the which was an other eſpeciall grace which God hath poured vppon your realmes. And euen as vnder King *Lucius*, It was the fiiſt part of the world, which did baniſh the Pagan Idolatrie, euen ſo God hath raiſed out of the ſame Iland, the ſaid *Conſtantine* the great, who expelled the ſame Romiſh Idolatry out of all the other Prouinces of the habitable world, whereof your Maieſtie hath a familiar example to imitate in this reſtorer of the Chriſtian religion.

This great *Conſtantine* your predeceſſor and countrieman, in the beginning of his Empire, *Hee ſtudied what God he ſhould chooſe*, as the ſame *Euſebius* ſaith, *that his Father had condemned the Error of Idolatrie, and al his life had worſhiped one onely God, the protector & guardien of the Empire, the free giuer of all good.*

Vppon this reſolution he made choiſe of the true God to ſerue, beleeuing that the onely cauſe of Kings and Emperours felicitie, proceeded from him alone, as the ſame Authour ſaith. *He worſhiped the ſame God that is aboue all things.* And in his ordinarie praiers, *beeing alone he ſpake to God alone.*

Whereby it appeareth that the religion which your Maieſtie hath eſtabliſhed in your realmes, is

con-

conformable to that of your predeceſſour *Conſtantine*, who worſhiped (as I haue ſaide) but one
onely God, the Creator of all things, and not the
Croſſe and Images of Ieſus Chriſt. In his ordinarie praiers hee did not call vppon the bleſſed
Virgin, Saint *Peter*, Saint *Paul*, nor the other Apoſtles and Martires, neyther haue we read that he
did conſecrate his Empire to Saint *Andrew* or
Saint *George*, as ſome of your predeceſſors in the
time of Error and blindeneſſe. *But did dedicate* Euſeb.ibid.
his houſe and familie to one King that is God onely.
God was his onely patron, *who recompenſed him
with all good things, and made him Lord and Con-
querour ouer all other Princes.* He commaunded all
his armie to call vppon one God, as the giuer of
victories, he appointed that in their praiers, *they
ſhould lift vp their handes to heauen, and the eyes of
their vnderſtanding to the moſt high king of Heauen:*
Hee alſo taught them the forme of praying to
God as followeth. *Wee confeſſe thee to be the onely God, wee acknowledge thee to be the onely King,
wee call vppon thee to aide vs* (they did not in-
uoke the virgin *Marie*) *by thee wee obtayne victorie
ouer our enemies, wee giue thee thankes for the benefites wee receiue in this preſent life, hoping for future
things by thy meanes : wee crye vnto thee with all
humilitie that it would pleaſe thee to make our
Emperour* Conſtantine *victorious, and preſerue
his Godly Children in long life and happie health.*

They

They did not call vpon the Angelles *Michael* and
Gabriel to giue them victory.

Hereby we fee that it is a falfe and flaundrous
thing, which the aduerfaries of the trueth im-
pute to your Maiefty to haue left the auncient
profeffion of your predeceffors, and to haue planted a new religion, begunne by *Martin Luther*,
Iohn Caluin and other moft learned men, whom
God hath ftirred vp in our age to abolifh the
falfe Romifh worfhippe, as hath beene fuffici-
ently prooued to your Maiefty in the difcour-
ces of the firft periode of the firft three hundred
yeeres. And to fhew that the onelye worfhippe
of the Creatour, without mingling the adoration
of the Creatures, continued vnto this fecond
periode of three hundred yeares in your Iland,
I will content my felfe with the faying of *Sedu-*
lius Scotus Hibernenfis, who lyued in the fift age,
in thefe wordes which hee hath drawne out of
Origen which I haue before cited. *It is a finne of*
Sedulius in *impietye to worfhippe anye other but the Father*
cap.1.epift *Sonne and holye Ghoft* . Whereunto Saint *Au-*
ad Rom. *guftine* fpeakes very fitly faying. *Know that the*
Chriftians, (whereof there is a Church in your
Towne) *Worfhippe not anye dead thing* , *neyther*
Aug.epift. *anye thing that hath beene made by God* , *but God*
45.ad Max *onelye is worfhipped* , *who hath made and created all*
grammat. *things.*
tom.2.

Our aduerfaries dare not affirme that the hoaft

. in

in the Maſſe is one of the three parſons of the Trinity, as we haue ſaide, which were a greater here-
ſie then that of *Arrius* , who ſayde that the
Sonne of God was a Creature, hauing a beginning, beeing not the Sonne of God from all
eternitye. All their Doctors teach that it is
made and created by the pronountiation of the
wordes of Ieſus Chriſt, taking his beginning by
the conſecration; whereby we inferre that they
are worſhippers of viſible formes, and therfore I-
dolaters in worſhipping it, ſeeing it is no eternall
creature, nor conſubſtantiall with God the Father: For *Athanaſius, Theodoret, Cyrillus* and all
the ancient Fathers, booth Greeke and Latine
of the ſecond periode of three hundred yeares
of Chriſtianity, teach, that if the Sonne of God
had beene created or had had any beginning, that
he had not beene worſhipped; for *that the Crea-*
ture dooth not worſhippe the Creature, God onely Athā. cont.
is to be worſhipped; if the Sonne had beene a creature he Arr. orat. 3
had not beene worſhipped, God forbidde we ſhould wor- et epiſt. ad
ſhippe the Creature , this madneſſe fittes beſt with Epheſ.
the Pagans, *and* Arrians. And in another place
hee ſaithe, that the Chriſtians worſhippe not
the body of Ieſus Chriſt deuided from the deity. Neither when wee worſhippe the worde
(ſaith hee) doe we ſeperate the worde from the
fleſh, but knowing that the worde hath beene
made fleſh , acknowledge that which is in the

fleſh,

flesh, to bee God. And a little after speaking of the Leaper he faith. *Hee worshipped the Lord in his body, and did acknowledge him for God* . And the same *Athanasius* teacheth vs, that the bodye of our Lorde is not consubstantiall with the Father, and therefore not to bee worshipped alone: with greater reason the hoaft, which cannot bee faide consubstantiall with the Father, is not to bee worshipped. For if the deitye of Iesus Chrift had not beene consubstantiall with the Father, and without beginning as the Father is, it had not beene lawfull to worshippe him. And this S I R E hath beene represented vnto you in the first periode, the which I repeate heere to shew the continuance of the worship of one onely God.

It is therefore manyfeft that the Christians of this second periode ending in the sixe hundred yeare of Christianity, did beleeue that it was a Pagan Idolatry to worshippe any Creature which had a beginning, restraining all adoration but to the Trinitye alone, worshipping nothing vnderneath it, the which is comprehended by *Gregorye Nazianzene* in few words, where he faith that we must worshippe nothing aboue or beneath the Trinity.

For faith hee, it is impossible to worshippe any thing aboue God ; and to worshippe anye thing vnderneath God is meere impietye. Let

Orat. 3. pro. pace.

vs

vs adde heereunto what *Theodoret* faith, (who liued in the fift age)touching the adoration of the Sacrament of the Lordes fupper, for that the Romains corrupting his writings,attributevnto him the worfhip of the Simbols of the body & bloud of our Lord Iefus Chrift,which he neuer dreampt of;for befides that which wee haue before alledged that hee condemned the *Arrians*, for that they worfhipped the deity, which they fayde was created; Hee faith in the fifty fiue queftion vppon *Genefis*, that God did allowe to eate the flefh of beaftes,to reftraine the people from worfhipping of them, forefeeing that men fhould fall into that blindeneffe and fuperftition as they fhould worfhippe beaftes, as wee reade of the worfhippe of the Golden Calfe like vnto the *Egyptians*; where *Theodoret* concludes, that it is a meere madneffe to worfhippe that which wee eate. So as according vnto *Theodoret* the priefts fhould bee madde to worfhippe that which they eate. *Athanafius* againft the *Arrians* teacheth, that the deity is not to be eaten, and yet the Romaines maintaine that their hoaft is God himfelfe and they finne that they eate that which is prefent in the hoaft, which in effect is to make the deity edible.

Our Sauiour before he left this world, would leaue vnto all men that fhould beleeue in him a perpetual comemoration of his true incarnation

E 4   and

and paſſion,to the end this memoriall ſhould bee, as it were a Simbole of the preſence of his humaine nature here on earth. He might as well after the manner of the Greekes and Romaines, haue left his portraite liuely drawne,to ſerue for a repreſentation and commemoration vnto ſuch as ſhould beleeue in him,yea they ſhould make infinite numbers of pictures, like vnto the ſtarres of heauen,to be in all aſſemblies of Chriſtians, and to ſhewe that he had put on a bodie like vnto thoſe pictures : but he who knewe the ſpirite of man commonly inclined to Idolatrie, would not leaue his repreſentation in the figure of a man, to take from him all ſubiect of Idolatrie, but hee choſe rather to inſtitute the Simboles in the Elements of bread and wine, wherewith his humaine nature was nouriſhed,as ours is now, the which is nouriſhed dayly, when there is no reaſon to worſhip them ſeeing we doe eate them, as *Theodoret* ſaith,& yet the ſpirit of darkenes,hauing in the olde time induced men to eate the beaſts, and then to worſhippe their Images, hath ſince found meanes to pull from the Church the firme breade in the Communion, bringing in *a kinde of wafer, which cannot properly bee called breade, beeing ſo thinne, on the which are printed the Images of Ieſus Chriſt*, the which they haue ſince worſhiped, whereas it was inſtituted onely to be eaten in remembrance that Ieſus Chriſt

Expoſitor ordin. in Rom.

Caſand.in Litur.

Honor.in Gemma a-nime.

had

had a humane bodie,nourifhed like vnto ours, to continue betwixt him and vs the communication of this incarnation, by the Elements wherewith we are all nourifhed.

This onely adoration of one God,hauing continued the fixe firft ages after our Sauiour. *Gregorie* the firft Bifhoppe of Rome brought in the inuocation of deade men in the beginning of the feauenth age, with many other fuperftitions : yet did he neuer teach that we muft worfhippe the Images of Iefus Chrift,as Chrift himfelfe , as *Thomas Aquinas* and other Romifh Doctors do teach vs,neither did he teach that we fhould worfhippe the confecrated Hoft as God , but contrariwife writing to *Serenus* Bifhoppe of *Marfeilles,* he commandes him in exprefle wordes, that he reftraine the people from the worfhip of Images, *and that the people fhould proftrate themfelues with all humilitie in the worfhip of the onely Almightie and holy Trinitie:* So as the Romifh doctrine of the laft ages, is directly contrarie to that of the firft fix ages after our Sauiour.

And yet this Pope commaunded them to hold Images in their Churches , yet not to worfhippe them,but to ferue as a commemoration vnto the people of the Hiftories of the Bible onely, but to what end ferued this ? It was as much as if they fhould forbid one to be drunke who is naturally inclined thereunto,& yet command him to lodge

in

in a Tauerne and to confort himfelfe with drunk-
ards, or like to him that fhould cōmaund a young
man in the heate of his youth, giuen to licentiouf-
neſſe, to abſtaine from it, and yet to lodge in a bro-
thell houſe. Mans nature is as much or more inclined to Idolatrie, then to drunkenneſſe or lux-
urie: & therefore the deuine prouidence knowing this imperfection in man, would take from him
all fubiect of Idolatrie. *Theodoret Serm. 7 de cur.*
Grec. affect. faith, That the wicked fpirit to deceiue
ignorant men, inuented the Arte of painting, g
uing, and other workemen to forge Images and
pictures to ferue for matter of Idolatrie: and that
they haue not onely filled the Temple with Images, but alfo the market places, ſtreetes, and publique places, yea euen rich mens houſes: the
which we fee practiſed at this day in the Temples,
markets, ſtreets and houſes of our aduerſaries. *Ar-*
nobius in the fixt booke againſt the Gentiles faith,
that they tooke the fame pretext for the vfe of I-
mages in their Churches. *To ferue the ignorant and*
vnruly people, whom they made to worfhip them,
giuing them venerable formes, to the end faith he,
they fhould beleeue there were fome vertue in their
brightneſſe, which did not onely dazle their eyes, but
ſtroke a terrour in their harts by the brightneſſe of their
reſplendent light.

Wee are to obferue the fpeciall grace which
God (continuing his worke) hath fhewed to the
Ilands

Ilands of great Britaine, in the beginning of this feauenth age : for *Gregorie* the firſt, hauing ſent *Auguſtine* the young, into the ſame Iland, to plant many ſuperſtitions,with the inuocation of Saints, neither he nor his doctrine were receiued, but the miſerie was, that ſoone after the death of *Gregorie,* the worſhipping of Images did ſo encreaſe, as it was the cauſe of many troubles betwixt the Weſt and the Eaſt, as we ſhall ſhew hereafter.

In the ſeauenth, eight, and ninth ages, making the third Period of Chriſtianiſme, the Hebrewe, Greeke, & Latine tongues were almoſt rooted out in the Weſterne parts of Europe, through the inundation of *Barbarians,* which did teare in peeces the Romain Empire,with the true diuinity: wherby we obſerue that euen as the true religion began with the ſaid Empire, and ſo encreaſed : euen ſo the Empire decaying, the ſinceritie of Chriſtian religion was almoſt aboliſhed, and declined ſo by their deuiſions in the Weſt, that Sathan working the miſtery of iniquitie in the harts of the Eaſterne Biſhoppes,made them to haue no reſpect to the purity of antiquity,bringing in a new worſhip of the Creatures,of the Croſſe,and of the Images of Ieſus Chriſt,the Apoſtles and Martires, an Idolatrie meerely Pagan.

We reade in the actes of the ſecond Councell of *Nice,* printed both in Greeke & Latine in *Paris,* that the ſaid Councell did decree, that we muſt

eſteeme

efteeme the image of Iefus Chrift, as Iefus Chrift himfelfe & that as the perfon of Iefus Chrift is diftinguifhed from that of the father in *hipoftafis*, and vnited in fubftance : euen fo his image fhould differ from him in fubftance and be vnited in perfon, the which is an intollerable blafphemy, and as great as the herefies of *Arrius* and *Neftorius* : for that were to make a God of a materiall thing or made by hand, and to worfhippe it as God, as the Gentiles did worfhippe the workemanfhippe of man.

At that fame time God raifed vp in the Iland of great *Brittaine*, that venerable *Beda,* who taught the Hebrew, Caldee, Greeke, and Latine tongues, Diuinity and Philofophy, out of whofe Schoole came *Iohannes Scotus* , and *Alcuinus* , who planted learning and the fciences in the Citty of Paris , & was afterwards fpread ouer al *Europe*. This *Iohannes Scotus* was Schoolemaifter to the Emperor *Charlemagne*, who withftood the idolatry of the Eaftern Churches, caufing the fecond counfell of *Nice* to be declared hereticall and abufiue ; by that of Francfort as we reade in *Ado viennenfis*. The fame Emperor became fo learned, as he writ a booke againft the Pagan worfhip of images, the which is found among the learned.

Out of the fame fchoole came one after another *Rhabanus Maurus* a Scotifhman , as many writers doe teftifie, *Claudius Taurinenfis* & *Bertram* a prieft, with

Ado.in Chro.

with other lights of the Church, in the third period of Chriſtianity, which are the ſeauenth eight and ninth ages, which haue fought againſt idolatry and the groſſe errors of the ſacrament, as wee ſhall hereafter ſhew.

The fourth period of Chriſtianiſme which containes the tenth, eleauenth, and twelfe ages, was ſo deſtitute of men adorned with true piety & learning, as the feedes of the Idolatry of former ages, came to the accompliſhment of the abhomination of diſſolution, at which time *Berengarius Archdeacon* of *Angers* with his diſciples, and *Peter de Valdo*, with the Schooles begun by him about the ſame periode, refiſted the Romiſh idolatry planted in all the Weſt.

We will likewiſe obſerue an eſpeciall grace, which God powred vpon your Ilands & realmes, during theſe ages of ignorance & idolatry, for euē as the great men of the former periode diſciples to the Engliſh *Beda* who maintained the onely worſhip of God went out of the Iland : euen ſo God during this fourth periode preſerued the ſame realmes, & defended them againſt the tyranny of Rome, for *Peter* of *Clugny* writing to *Bernard*, faith, that the *Scotiſhmen* in his time did celebrate, their Eaſter after the Greeke manner, which is a teſtimony they were not yet ſubiect to the church of Rome, which held thē heretickes that followwed the cerimonies of the Greekes, who in the

time

time of the said *Bernard* had their *Lyturgie* and feruice of the Church, as they haue at this day, which
is a communion like vnto that of the reformed
Church of thefe times : neither did the Greeke
Church euer allow of that heatheniſh worſhippe
of the Sacrament of the Lordes ſupper as in the
Romiſh Church, which caufed *Marcus Epheſi-
us* (who was Orator for the Greekes at the counfell of *Florence* in a fermon printed at *Paris* in
Greeke and *Latine*, at the ende of the volume of
Lyturgies) to confute the Maffe of the *Latines*,
as directly contrary to the inftitution of Iefus
Chrift.

So as the *Scottiſhmen* who maintained the ceremonies of the Greeke Churches, had not yet
receiued the new Romiſh Maffe, nor the heathen
adoration of the hoaft, whereby we fee that the
people of your realmes were the firft that made
publike profeffion of Chrift, and aboliſhed Gen-
tilifme, during the cruell perfecutions of Romiſh
Emperours, and when as the tyranny of the Biſhops of Rome, brought into the Church about
400. yeares fince the worſhip of the hoaft, as God
the Creator, the fame Britiſh people were alfo
the laft of the Weft part of *Europe*, which r cei-
ued the abominable worſhip of things created in-
fteede of the Creator.

This heatheniſh worſhip began vnder Pope
Honorius 3. about the yeare 1225. who comman-
ded

ded all Prieftes and Curats to teach the people to
kneele at the Eleuation of the hoaft in the Maffe,
or when it fhould be carried to ficke perfons; yet
this idolatry was not long after receiued in the
Churches of *Germanie* and *France*. For *Ralfe de
Riuo* printed a booke at Rome. *de Can.obfer propof.*
22. witneffing that *Nicholas. 3.* about the yeare
1277. tooke the olde miffalles out of all Churches
of Rome bringing in a new forme of Maffe inuented by the Fryers minors , or *Francifcans:*
At this day (faith hee) *all the bookes at Rome
are new after the manner of Saint* Francis, and mea-
ning to difcribe the forme of Maffe obferued in
thofe dayes in *Germany* , *France* & other nations ,
hee faith. Leauing the manner of the Fryers minors, *let vs follow the holy Canons , the ancient Scriptures, and the generall cuftomes of places, and in doubt-
full things the moft auncient bookes* . And in the
twenty three propofition he defcribes particular-
ly all the ceremonies of the Maffe , as it was vfed
in his time , who liued in the beginning of the
foreteenth age of Chriftianifme , at what time it
is found that the coniunction of the Bread and
Wine was obferued according to the inftitution of our Sauiour , and that both the Prieft
and people did eate and drinke togeather
ftanding , without adoration or inuocation
of the Sacramentes : and in the ende of the
faide propofition hee faithe . *It is facriledge*

to vſe bread onely dipt in wine in the Sacrament of the Communion. So as there was no difference betwixt the Communion of the reformed Church, and the Communion of the Maſſe in thoſe daies, except the ſigne of the Croſſe, and ſome other ceremonies, veſtaments and incenſe. The Maſſe therfore of our age, is a new fiction of Cordiliers or Franciſcan Friars, & the worſhip of a pretended God, and the priuation of the cup is a plaine ſacriledge: for if they abuſe to vſe bread ſteept in wine inſtead of following the ful inſtitutiō of our Sauiour, was (as they ſaid *Rodolphus de Riuo* writeth) condemned as ſacriledge, with greater reaſon, is it a more horrible ſacriledge to haue quite taken away the vſe of the wine from the people. The Romiſh Church of our age, cannot bee called the true Church, ſeeing they haue no Communion of the Cuppe, and are fallen from the true Prieſthoode: as the *Arrians* and *Neſtorians* by their errours loſt the outward markes of Prieſthoode.

During the fift Period of the ages of Chriſtianiſme, which contains the thirteenth, fourteenth, and fifteenth ages, the Weſterne Church was deuided into two parts: for in the time of *Bernard, Peter de Valdo,* a rich Bourgeſſe of *Lions,* hauing beene inſtructed in the onely worſhippe of God by the reading of the holy Scriptures, had the Romiſh Idolatrie in ſuch horror, as he ſould all his goods, and cauſed the Bible and many writings of
the

the auncient fathers to be tranflated into French,
he made affemblies at *Lions*, and appointed penfi-
ons for religious learned men to fet vp Schooles
of diuinitie, who beeing fince perfecuted by the
Popes and their adherents, the faid Schooles were
difperfed ouer all France, and a good part of
Spaine, Germanie, and Bohemia, who haue euer
fince maintained the fame articles of the faith,
which are profeffed at this day in the Churches
of your realmes, whereof fome were called *Al-
bigeois*, and others *Taborites*, which haue florifhed
and raigned vnto this day, notwithftanding all
the perfecutions, fires, flames, and cruell tor-
ments vfed againft them by the fupporters and fa-
uourers of Rome.

Out of this Schoole alfo came *Iohn Hus*, and *Ie-
rofme* of *Prage*, *Wickliffe* an Englifhman, *Paul Crau*
a Scottifh man, who maintained the true and
onely worfhippe of one onely God, and other
articles of the faith, confeffed by the reformed
Churches of Europe, the which is feene by the
articles recited by *Æneas Siluius*, (beeing fince
Pope) which fhewes a notable correfpondencie
betwixt the firft Period of Chriftianifme and the
fift : for euen as in the firft three hundred yeeres
the true Chriftians who worfhipped one onely
God, without mingling the adoration of Creatures had beene perfecuted by Pagan Rome, euen
fo the worfhippers of this true adoration haue
beene

*Acneas Sil-
uius in Hift.
Boem.*

G

beene cruelly perfecuted during the three hundred yeres of the fift Period, by Roome difguifed with a Chriftian maske.

There is an other admirable correfpondencie betwixt thefe and the fecond Period, for euen as in the end of the fiift Period, the God of armies did raife vp that great *Conftantine* to plant his Church by force throughout all the Romaine Empire, beeing then Pagan, abolifhing Idolatrie in the worfhip of men, of Images, and of vifible and material formes: euen fo after the end of this fift Period, God fuffered the reftoring of the faid true auncient & Chriftian religion to be done by armes We read in the Bohemian Hiftorie of the faid *Æneas Siluius*, that *Zifca* a great Captaine affembled in the yeere 1501. a mightie armie, beating downe all Idols and Images, abolifhing the new Maffe, or the woifhiping of the Hoaft. Soone after many Princes did rife, and many faithfull learned men by whofe miniftrie and valour, the pureneffe of the preaching of the Gofpell was reftored in the finceritie of Chriftian truth, as it was at the comming of *Conftantine* in the Weft of Europe.

I may therefore iuftly fay, that among all the Princes which haue laboured for the reftoring and reformation of the auncient Church, your predeceffours King *Edward*, and Queene *Eliza-beth*, (of happie memories) haue beene the firft which

43

which haue built vpon this foundation after *Conftantine,*(although long after) and now (S I R E)
thefe bleffed foules behould from heauen the full
perfection of their worke which muft be finifhed
by you, whom they haue left the fucceffour and
heire of their moft royall enterprifes.

Your Maieftie hath a familiar example in the
life of the difceafed Queene,(of happie memorie)
who hath bene a true mother vnto you: In whofe
gouernment we haue feene as in a looking glaffe,
that God hath accompanied her with an admirable and extraordinarie profperitie, fœlicitie, and
happie fucceffe in all her affaires : for hee hath
drawne her from a prifon to a kingdome, he hath
made her to raigne fortie and fiue yeeres in
great peace and tranquilitie, hauing difcouered
aboue twentie enterprifes readie to bee put in
execution againft her life and ftate : hee indued
her with all kindes of perfections and vertues, as
prudence,modeftie, and wifdome in all her actions,beautified with a liuely and found iudgement
farre exceeding her fex. And for a fulneffe of
happineffe, the fame God did prolong her daies
vnto threefcore and ten yeares, in the which fhe
was alwayes victorious ouer her enemies,
both home-bred and ftrangers . What is then
the caufe (S I R E) I will attribute it wholy
vnto God, and to the puritie of his Gofpell,
and to Chriftian religion the which fhe hath eftablifhed

blifhed in her kingdoms, whereof this moft Chriftian and generous Princeffe made a fincere profeffion all her life. Hauing therefore in this peace-
able and Chriftianlike manner yeelded vp her
bleffed foule to her benefactor and Creatour the
great God immortall,fhe left thofe realmes aboū-
ding in all riches,in great peace and admirable v-
nion and concord. And moreouer to feale vp her
forepaffed life and death with a greater benefit,
for the loue fhe bare vnto her fubiectes which is a
great proofe of the bleffing of God, we haue
feene the wifdome fhe vfed euen at the laft gafpe,
hauing fo profitably and fo effectually perfwa-
ded her fubiects to imbrace & acknowledge your
Maiefty whom fhe knew to be the true lawfull &
vndoubted heire and fucceffor of her goodly &
flourifhing Realmes of *England*, and *Ireland*, by
right of confanguinity and lawfull fucceffion.
Who dooth not fee the affiftance of God in all
this action ? In that he would haue your Maiefty
eftablifhed in this moft high degree of honour,
not for any other refpect,but that in raigning happily and in peace,you fhould finifh the full deliuery and reftoring of Ifrael, and of the Churches
of your realmes ; and to continue the pure preaching of the Gofpel,fo happily begun by her Maiefty (of bleffed and happy memory)againft the I-
dolatry of Rome. I doubt not(S I R E)but Sathan
and his fupporters will herein imploy their ftrata-
gems

gems to counfell your Maiefty, & to induce you
to ioyne with that great whore of *Babilon*, a whore
which makes the kings & princes of the earth drūk
with the cup of her fpiritual fornicatiō. But I affure
my felfe that your Maiefty (like vnto wary & nice
Vliffes) will ftop your eares againft al her charmes,
inchantments and allurements continuing inuio-
lable, conftant and refolute in your royall vertues,
the which God hath bountifully planted in you,
to maintaine and preferue his Church and Sacraments (to his honor and glory) in their purety, a-
gainft the poifons & Romifh inuenfions of men.
Moft humbly befeeching your Maiefty to remem-
ber that the * Popes pretend to be the true kings ** Matth.*
of *England* and *Ireland* houlding the Kinges of *Paris in*
the faid kingdoms for their vaffals and tributaries, *Hift. Angl,*
fub. Henric,
who now vnder colour to free you from their faid *3.pa.660.*
pretenfions, would draw you vnto them, and im- *Mat. vveft-*
mon in Flo-
pofe vpon you a moft heauy and feruile yoake. If *rib. hift. fub.*
your Maiefty fhould fo forget your felfe as to *an.1216.*
cleaue vnto them, who knoweth not that their
fucceffors are accuftomed to difanull the deedes
and promifes of their predeceffors, and which is
more to hould no faith with heretickes as they
call you? But (S I R E) this is nothing in refpect of
the hard flauery of foules, whom they torture
with their cenfures and excommunications. So
as you fhal no fooner fubiect your felfe vnto their
lawes, but vpon the firft diflike, they will abfolue
and

and free your ſubiects from their oath of obedience due vnto their true and lawfull King, they
will depoſe you at their pleaſures, and giue your
crownes to whom they like, wherof we haue too
many late examples. But when they ſhall ſee your
Maieſty to oppoſe conſtantly againſt their tyranny, they will not dare to attempt againſt you nor
your realmes. And moreouer is not your Maieſty
at this preſent protector of the Church of all your
realmes? yea the greateſt of the Soueraigne kings
which profeſſe the purenes of the Goſpell? ſhall
not theſe lawfull titles of honour be ſufficient to
diuert your Maieſty from following the counſell
of ſuch Sirens of ſtate? They would gladly per-
ſwade you to acknowledge this furious beaſt, who
ſeekes but to deuour good Kings, & to chalenge
to himſelfe all power (as he ſaith) in heauen, earth
and hell. An eſſentiall marke that he is the man of
iniquity (mētioned in the Scriptures) which hath
raiſed himſelfe aboue all nations, and aboue all religion. If this monſter held you at his deuoticn,
(the which I with all your good ſubiects thinke to
be impoſſible, how great a leuiathan ſoeuer he be)
doubt not (S I R E) but he would make you the
moſt vile and moſt abiect of al his lifetenants, trea-
ding you more proudly vnder his feete, then euer
he did the good Emperour *Barbaroſſe*. And then
let your Maieſty conſider in what miſery, calami-
ty and deſolation of deſolations both you my
Lord

Lord the Prince (whom you loue deerely) and all
your fubiects who pray for you hourely, fhould
be reduced in thefe your flourifhing realmes.

The Almighty God which gouerneth & difpo-
feth of Monarchies according to his will, which
giueth victories in battailes, who is the fpring
and fountaine of all wifedome and knowledge,
giue your Maiefty a raigne like vnto the Queene
of bleffed & happy memory. Increafe your Maiefty in wifedome and knowledge, and in true piety and purenefle of his feruice: giue you victory
ouer all them that fhall attempt againft you or
your eftate; and fmifh the worke in you begun for
the reftoring of the true Church, banifhing out
of your Ilands and realmes, all tyranny, herefie
and Romifh Idolatry. And for a happy ende,
the fame eternall God giue you a full and perfect inioying of the Crowne of glory in
the happineffe of eternall life
through his fonne Iefus
Chrift our Lorde.

FINIS.